PIANO · VOCAL · CHORDS

≡ THE COLE PORTER SONG COLLECTION ≡

VOLUME ONE: 1912–1936

Cole Porter in the early 193[...]

Photos and research assist[...]
The Cole Porter Collecti[...]
American Musical Theatre[...]
and the Cole Porter Music [...]y Trusts, Peter Felcher, Trustee,
and Roberta Staats, Executive Director.

Produced by
Alfred Music Publishing Co., Inc.
P.O. Box 10003
Van Nuys, CA 91410-0003
alfred.com

Printed in USA.

ISBN-10: 0-7390-6230-1
ISBN-13: 978-0-7390-6230-2

Contents

TITLE	SHOW/FILM (YEAR)	PAGE
The Songs of Cole Porter		4
After You, Who?	Gay Divorce (1932)	32
All Through the Night	Anything Goes (1934)	36
Anything Goes	Anything Goes (1934)	21
Begin the Beguine	Jubilee (1935) / Broadway Melody of 1940 (1940)	42
Blow, Gabriel, Blow	Anything Goes (1934)	49
Buddie, Beware	Anything Goes (1934)	56
Don't Look at Me That Way	Paris (1928)	62
Down in the Depths (On the 90th Floor)	Red, Hot and Blue! (1936)	66
Easy to Love	Born to Dance (1936)	72
Experiment	Nymph Errant (1933)	76
Goodbye, Little Dream, Goodbye	O Mistress Mine (1936)	80
The Great Indoors	The New Yorkers (1930)	84
How Could We Be Wrong?	Nymph Errant (1933)	88
How's Your Romance?	Gay Divorce (1932)	92
I Get a Kick Out of You	Anything Goes (1934)	98
I Happen to Like New York	The New Yorkers (1930)	103
I'm in Love Again	Greenwich Village Follies of 1924 (1924)	107
I'm Unlucky at Gambling	Fifty Million Frenchmen (1929)	110
It's Bad for Me	Nymph Errant (1933)	114
It's De-Lovely	Red, Hot and Blue! (1936)	118
I've a Shooting Box in Scotland	See America First (1916)	124
I've Got You on My Mind	Star Dust (1931) / Gay Divorce (1932)	130
I've Got You Under My Skin	Born to Dance (1936)	134
Just One of Those Things	Jubilee (1935)	140
The Laziest Gal in Town	Stage Fright (1950)	146
Let's Do It (Let's Fall in Love)	Paris (1928)	151
Let's Misbehave	(*cut from* Paris, 1928)	156
Longing for Dear Old Broadway	The Pot of Gold (1912)	160
Looking at You	Wake Up and Dream (1929)	163
Love for Sale	The New Yorkers (1930)	168
Miss Otis Regrets	Hi Diddle Diddle (1934)	174
Mister and Missus Fitch	Gay Divorce (1932)	177
Night and Day	Gay Divorce (1932)	181
Old-Fashioned Garden	Hitchy-Koo of 1919 (1919)	186

Contents

TITLE	SHOW/FILM (YEAR)	PAGE
Ours	Red, Hot and Blue! (1936)	191
The Physician	Nymph Errant (1933)	196
Ridin' High	Red, Hot and Blue! (1936) / High Society (1956)	201
Take Me Back to Manhattan	The New Yorkers (1930)	206
The Tale of the Oyster	Fifty Million Frenchmen (1929)	220
They All Fall in Love	The Battle of Paris (1929)	215
Wake Up and Dream	Wake Up and Dream (1929)	211
Weren't We Fools?	(written for Fanny Brice, 1927)	228
What Is This Thing Called Love?	Wake Up and Dream (1929)	232
Where Have You Been?	The New Yorkers (1930)	236
Which?	Wake Up and Dream (1929)	240
Why Shouldn't I?	Jubilee (1935)	244
You Do Something to Me	Fifty Million Frenchmen (1929)	248
You Don't Know Paree	Fifty Million Frenchmen (1929)	225
You're the Top	Anything Goes (1934)	256
You've Got That Thing	Fifty Million Frenchmen (1929)	252

Cole Porter in a celebratory mood with Betty Sherlin Smith, in an undated photo from the early 1930s.

The Songs of Cole Porter

In the annals of American popular song, no works embody a writer's personality more than those written by Cole Porter (1891–1964). Sophisticated and sly, romantic and sentimental, witty, impish, bawdy, and sometimes downright naughty, Porter's songs never fail to delight, surprise, and entertain audiences. In an era when most songwriters wrote either words or music, Porter did both, drawing from a seemingly bottomless reservoir of gorgeous melodies and erudite, ingenious lyrics. Although rhyming dictionaries were part of his songwriting arsenal, many of the words Porter employed were made up, twisted, or distorted to suit his purposes. Sometimes a word was deliberately mispronounced in order to fit the rhyme. Porter didn't care. The English language was his plaything.

He used proper names from popular culture more effectively, and more frequently, than anyone. His songs are littered with casual references to the cultural icons of his day: personalities from motion pictures, politics, literature, sports, and high society. His sense of humor is always playful and never mean-spirited. It became a badge of honor to have one's name mentioned in a Cole Porter lyric.

The emotions in a Cole Porter song run the gamut; they can be giddy and playful, unabashedly optimistic, or intensely passionate. His melodies are often underappreciated in comparison with his memorable lyrics, but in cases such as "Night and Day," the music and lyrics are equally brilliant.

Cole Porter was born in Peru, Indiana, on June 9, 1891, with the proverbial silver spoon in his mouth. The family fortune came from his grandfather, J.O., through investments in farmland that produced rich deposits of coal and oil. Although Porter and his father, Sam, were not close, he did have a long and intimate relationship with his mother, Kate.

While still a small boy, Porter began taking piano lessons. In the summer months, he was a popular attraction at Lake Maxinkuckee, an Indiana resort where he entertained onboard the steamer *Peerless*. After graduating from boarding school in 1909, he enrolled at Yale College, where his innate songwriting talent began to blossom. He excelled at writing football fight songs; his composition "Bull Dog" became a perennial favorite and is still sung at campus athletic events.

Porter as a teenager, when he attended Worcester Academy boarding school in Massachusetts. He started there in 1905 and graduated in 1909.

At Yale, Porter joined the Yale Glee Club, eventually becoming its president. He developed a popular solo act in which he showed off original compositions and vaudeville-inspired humorous patter. Most important, he began writing musical comedies for his fraternity, Delta Kappa Epsilon, and also for the Yale Dramat. This proved to be the beginning of not only a Yale tradition, but also Porter's long career as a songwriter for theatre and, eventually, motion pictures.

The arrangements in this book are taken from the original sheet music editions of Cole Porter's works, which have been re-engraved for easier reading. Wherever possible, we have included the complete lyrics, including rarely performed additional refrains. The arrangements as well as the selection of songs have been approved by the Porter Trusts, making these two volumes the most authoritative representation of the greatest works of Cole Porter.

Longing for Dear Old Broadway

The Pot of Gold was one of four shows scored by Cole Porter while he was a student at Yale University. Unpublished until 1975, the song "Longing for Dear Old Broadway" was written in 1912 during his senior year, and is the first of many songs Porter wrote in tribute to New York City. The show was performed once at his fraternity house and again at the Hotel Taft in New Haven. Although the song doesn't sparkle with the same wit of his later works, it shows evidence of his attraction to the bright lights and excitement that goes along with the world of the theatre and the lifestyle of the privileged.

I've a Shooting Box in Scotland

After Porter graduated from Yale, he enrolled at Harvard Law School, where he soon transferred to the School of Music. In 1914, with the witty songs of Gilbert and Sullivan in his head, Porter wrote "I've a Shooting Box in Scotland." This classic "list song" was written for *Paranoia*, a show Porter had planned while still at Yale. In 1916, he revised the song for the show *See America First*. The song, with its multiple references to exotic place names, would prove to be prophetic, since Porter would spend much of his life "collecting" country homes during his many travels across the globe. *See America First* only lasted 15 performances, but it launched Cole Porter's Broadway career. "I've a Shooting Box in Scotland" was also the first Porter song to be commercially recorded; in 1916, an instrumental version by Joseph C. Smith and His Orchestra was recorded for the Victor record label.

Old-Fashioned Garden

Porter's first big hit would not have been written without the generosity of impresario Florenz Ziegfeld. The legendary producer realized that he had some leftover flower costumes from his latest revue, so he gave them to producer Charles Dillingham. Dillingham was working on a revue of his own titled *Hitchy-Koo of 1919,* named in honor of its comedian-star, Ray Hitchcock. Hitchcock then asked Porter to write a song to show off the colorful costumes. The result was "Old-Fashioned Garden," which became the show's hit and sold over a hundred thousand sheet music copies. British horticulturists, however, sniffed with derision at Porter's lyrics, which detailed a garden consisting of flowers that could not possibly grow in the same place at the same time of year.

I'm in Love Again

After *Hitchy-Koo of 1919* closed, Porter married Linda Lee Thomas (1883–1954) and moved to Paris, where the newlyweds bought an elegant home near the Eiffel Tower. Porter had met Thomas at a wedding reception at Paris's Ritz Hotel; she had served at the American Aviation Headquarters during World War I. Although they spent much of their marriage traveling, the Porters called the Paris residence home until 1937. While there, Porter studied counterpoint, harmony, and orchestration as he tried to find his own unique voice. His work for much of the 1920s was sporadic and mostly inconsequential until the 1928 breakthrough hit, *Paris.*

In 1924, John Murray Anderson hired Porter to write songs for the fifth annual edition of his *Greenwich Village Follies.* A revue of visual extravagance, the show starred vaudeville's blackface comic duo Moran and Mack (The Two Black Crows), the singing Dolly Sisters, and Vincent Lopez's dance orchestra. The show was so top-heavy with material that on opening night, the first act didn't end until 11:00. "Beautiful and dumb" was how *New York Sun* critic Alexander Woollcott described the show. Many changes were made before it went on the road. Unfortunately, all of Cole Porter's songs were among the casualties. In 1925, T.B. Harms published one of the discarded numbers, "I'm in Love Again." The song became a hit in 1927 when it was subsequently recorded by Paul Whiteman and His Orchestra, the nation's most popular dance band. The recording features one of the earliest vocals by Bing Crosby.

Marlene Dietrich singing "The Laziest Gal in Town," from *Stage Fright* (1950).

The Laziest Gal in Town

Another Porter song that had an afterlife was "The Laziest Gal in Town." Written in 1927 for a summer show at Edmond Sayag's Ambassadeurs Café, it was revived by director Alfred Hitchcock for his 1950 film *Stage Fright.* In the movie, the song is sung by flamboyant stage actress Charlotte Inwood (Marlene Dietrich). The number became a signature song for Dietrich and is famously parodied by Madeline Kahn in Mel Brooks's Western spoof, *Blazing Saddles.*

Weren't We Fools?

Comedienne and vaudeville star Fanny Brice met Cole Porter in 1926 at the Ca' Rezzonico, a lavish palazzo the Porters rented in Venice. Porter had been distraught over his sagging fortunes as a Broadway songwriter, but when Brice asked him to write two songs for her upcoming vaudeville show, he agreed. One of the two, a deeply affecting torch song called "Weren't We Fools?" was ideal for Brice, who had recently divorced gambler Nicky Arnstein. On November 21, 1927, Brice sang the song on the first night of an engagement at Broadway's Palace Theatre. On the second night, however, Arnstein showed up in the audience, and Brice, still tormented by their breakup, refused to perform it. She never sang it again.

In 2000, the American Ballet Theater presented a ballet by choreographer Christian Holder called *Weren't We Fools?* which consisted of Cole Porter songs, arranged and orchestrated by Judy Brown.

Don't Look at Me That Way

In 1928, after more than a decade of writing songs for mediocre revues, Porter was ready to give up on his dream of being a success on Broadway. Producer E. Ray Goetz was starring his wife, Irene Bordoni, in a new show called *Paris* and asked Porter if he could write some saucy American songs with a French twist for Bordoni to sing. Goetz's former brother-in-law, Irving Berlin, told Goetz that Porter knew Paris better than any American songwriter. Bordoni was one of the theatre world's top stars, and she used her coquettish sex appeal to great effect in shows such as George Gershwin's *The French Doll,* in which she sang the risqué "Do It Again." Her coy delivery worked perfectly on Porter's "Don't Look at Me That Way," in which she sang the wonderfully constructed line "My will is strong, but my won't is weak."

Let's Do It (Let's Fall in Love)

"Don't Look at Me That Way" was a good song, but it paled in comparison to a number that catapulted Porter to fame: "Let's Do It (Let's Fall in Love)." Although the pronoun "it" was used coyly, it was apparent to all what Porter was referring to. The sly, clever lyrics were ideally suited for Irene Bordoni's character and image. Introduced by Bordoni and Arthur Margetson, "Let's Do It" became the biggest hit from *Paris,* and was the first of Porter's many "list" songs to become a showstopper. Its extra refrains were kept in reserve for when overwhelming audience enthusiasm demanded more. In all, Porter wrote five refrains, each focusing on a zoological category. The song is a veritable study of the mating habits of the Earth's creatures, including everything from jellyfish to locusts.

Let's Misbehave

In the summer of 1927, Irving Aaronson and His Commanders, one of New York's top dance bands, premiered Cole Porter's "Let's Misbehave" at the Ambassadeurs Café in Paris. They recorded it for Victor later that year, with Phil Saxe providing the vocal. The song was so successful that Aaronson and his band were hired to perform it in Porter's *Paris;* by the time the show made its debut on Broadway, the song had been replaced by "Let's Do It," presumably because the latter song treated sex more ambiguously. Despite its excision, "Let's Misbehave" was featured in the 1927 edition of *The Ziegfeld Follies,* in which it was sung to great acclaim by Cliff Edwards (a.k.a "Ukulele Ike"), whose visage graces the song's sheet music edition. It remains a popular Porter vehicle, used by director Woody Allen in the soundtrack to two of his films: *Everything You Always Wanted to Know About Sex* and *Bullets over Broadway.* Despite the overwhelming success of the song that replaced "Let's Misbehave," the brilliance of such lines as "If you want a future, darling / Why don't you get a past?" cannot be overlooked.

Irene Bordoni with Irving Aaronson and His Commanders, featured in *Paris* (1928).

Which?

Another song dropped from *Paris* before the New York opening was "Which?" a song of indecision that was probably written with Irene Bordoni in mind. It was inexplicably taken out of the score, only to resurface in the 1929 revue *Wake Up and Dream,* sung by Jessie Matthews. *Wake Up and Dream* made its debut in London in March, and was noteworthy for its opulent use of 24 sets and 500 costumes. The show did well, with 263 performances in London beginning in March followed by another 136 in New York starting in December. Its success was most likely hindered by both the stock market crash in October and competition from another Porter hit, *Fifty Million Frenchmen,* which had already been playing for a month.

Wake Up and Dream

The title number from *Wake Up and Dream* is one of several philosophical songs Porter wrote throughout his career. In these songs, which include "Experiment" and "Use Your Imagination," Porter sets aside his rapier wit and sardonic cultural references to adopt a more wistful, thoughtful tone. It is almost as if he is directing his message inward instead of to his audience. The song reflects Porter's own carefree attitude to seize the day and set aside everyday worries. The song was introduced in London by tenor George Metaxa and in New York by Jessie Matthews.

Looking at You

Cole Porter wrote "Looking at You" for Clifton Webb to sing in *La Revue des Ambassadeurs in Paris*, featuring the Noble Sissle orchestra. Webb sang the song so well that Porter added it to the score of *Wake Up and Dream.* It was introduced in London and on Broadway by Jessie Matthews. Although the song is meant to be performed by a man, audiences did not object to Matthews singing it, a fact that reflects the period's flexibility with regard to gender in song lyrics.

What Is This Thing Called Love?

In his autobiography, *Musical Stages*, composer Richard Rodgers tells of his conversation with Cole Porter in which Porter said he had discovered the secret of writing hit songs. Rodgers recalls, "As I breathlessly awaited the magic formula, he leaned over and confided, 'I'll write Jewish tunes.' " Few songs in Porter's repertoire exhibit this notion better than the hit song from *Wake Up and Dream,* "What Is This Thing Called Love?" Introduced by Elsie Carlisle in England and Frances Shelley in New York, the song's haunting melody, which moves unexpectedly from minor to major keys, was compared to melodies found in the Jewish liturgy. (Porter once claimed he got the melody from a native dance in Marrakesh, Morocco.) Columnist Walter Winchell called it "the most whistley and contagious Cole Porter tune yet." Leo Reisman and His Orchestra recorded it, with a vocal by Lew Conrad and a growling, muted trumpet solo by Bubber Miley of the Duke Ellington Orchestra. The song became a standard that was also popular with bebop musicians, who used the unusual chord progressions as the basis for such songs as "Hot House" by Tadd Dameron and "Barry's Bop" by Fats Navarro.

Gertrude Lawrence in the film *The Battle of Paris* (1929).

They All Fall in Love

With the success of *Paris*, Hollywood began to take notice of Cole Porter's work. Talking pictures were still novelties, and producers were on the lookout for entertaining songs to feature in their films. In November 1929, Paramount Pictures hired Porter to write two songs for British stage actress Gertrude Lawrence to sing in the film *The Battle of Paris.* "They All Fall in Love" is in the same category as "Let's Do It," except that its message is more mischievous than salacious. With the stock market crash freshly in his mind, Porter takes a wry poke at Wall Street:

> You may believe your broker
> Is very mediocre
> At playing with your stocks and bonds.
> At business he may blunder,
> Yet he's a perfect wonder
> When he plays with blondes.

Due to a rushed production schedule and a vapid, uninteresting script, *The Battle of Paris* was a dismal failure. Described by one critic as approaching a "floperetta," the movie nevertheless provided Porter with his first screen credit.

You Do Something to Me

Porter's production following *The Battle of Paris* was the musical *Fifty Million Frenchmen*, which fared better. Produced by E. Ray Goetz, who had worked with Porter on *Paris*, the show opened three days before *The Battle of Paris.* Reviews were good and it became a hit, spurred by a ringing endorsement from Goetz's former brother-in-law, Irving Berlin, whom Goetz originally wanted to write the score. When Berlin saw that the story concerned decadent bohemians in Paris, however, he knew it was right up Cole Porter's alley. The show's lighter-than-air plot has to do with an impetuous American playboy (William Gaxton) who wagers that he can make a young girl (Genevieve Tobin) fall in love with him in a month's time without using his extensive financial resources.

Porter's score includes 20 songs, half the number he had submitted to Goetz. Most of the songs skillfully define the characters' moods and personalities, making *Fifty Million Frenchmen* an early example of an integrated score. The most famous song from the show is "You Do Something to Me," a love-at-first-sight song sung by Peter Forbes (Gaxton) to Looloo Carroll (Tobin). The song's most celebrated lyric shows Porter's ingenious ability to repeat the same vowel six times in one line: "Do do that voodoo that you do so well."

William Gaxton and Genevieve Tobin in
Fifty Million Frenchmen (1929).

I'm Unlucky at Gambling

Introduced by Evelyn Hoey in *Fifty Million Frenchmen*, "I'm Unlucky at Gambling" features Porter's outrageously inventive rhymes in the song's first verse, while retaining more conventional rhyming lines for the refrain. The verse rhymes "day" and "play" with "straightaway" and "croupier," while the refrain includes the oft-used "love" and "above." The second verse, which is not included in the original published sheet music, contains one of Porter's few references to homosexuality in his songs.

You Don't Know Paree

"You Don't Know Paree" is a wistful and beautiful number sung by William Gaxton that implies Cole Porter's reluctance to leave Paris and return to New York. The song replaced "The Snake in the Grass," a brief ballet from *Fifty Million Frenchmen*'s tryout period in Boston. "You Don't Know Paree" appeared in time for the show's New York premiere. In the song, Paris is identified as a wondrous city for tourists, but "Paree" is for those who live there and understand the city that sleeps beneath the surface, where "the laughter hides the tears." After her divorce from E. Ray Goetz, Irene Bordoni included the song in her solo nightclub act.

You've Got That Thing

Porter's penchant for metaphorical comparisons is highlighted in "You've Got That Thing," which was sung as a duet in *Fifty Million Frenchmen* by Jack Thompson and Betty Compton. Next to "You Do Something to Me," this is the most popular number in the show. The song continues the coy, suggestive theme introduced in "Let's Do It" the previous year. Once again, Porter playfully skirts around the unspoken word "sex," which is implied in nearly every line. The lyrics include references to historically amorous couples such as Adam and Eve, and Samson and Delilah, but also contain a contemporary reference, rhyming "those taking ways" with "Cartier's."

Betty Compton and Jack Thompson
singing "You've Got That Thing," from
Fifty Million Frenchmen (1929).

The Tale of the Oyster

Despite the racy lyrics of some of Porter's songs, the most controversial number in *Fifty Million Frenchmen* is a simple tale about a simple organism, sung by American tourist Violet Hildegarde (comedienne Helen Broderick). Porter wrote "The Tale of the Oyster" (originally titled "The Scampi") as a satire of German lieder and performed it to amuse his friends on the Lido in Venice. The song is a humorous trifle about an oyster that yearns to see how the upper set lives and is swallowed by Mrs. Hoggenheimer, a jewel-encrusted dowager lunching at the Park Casino. After leaving on her yacht, the unfortunate matron gets seasick and returns the oyster to the sea in a most unbecoming manner. The song earned the wrath of critic Gilbert Seldes, who pronounced the number "disgusting," prompting its removal from the score. In 1965, the song itself was regurgitated (as was the hapless oyster) by producer Ben Bagley for his revue *The Decline and Fall of the Entire World as Seen Through the Eyes of Cole Porter.* It was sung with great élan by Kaye Ballard.

Take Me Back to Manhattan

At the end of 1930, Porter followed *Fifty Million Frenchmen* with a satire called *The New Yorkers.* Based on the drawings of *The New Yorker* staff artist Peter Arno, the show is filled with beguiling songs celebrating life in the Big Apple. Described by one critic as "one of the merriest, maddest musical comedies of recent issue," it deals lightheartedly with the upper crust and sordid underbelly of New York life: Park Avenue matrons, bootleggers, gangsters, and prostitutes. (The most famous line from the show is "Park Avenue—the street where bad women walk good dogs.") Playing against such smash hits as *Girl Crazy*, *Three's a Crowd*, and *Fine and Dandy*, *The New Yorkers* was the top seller, and might have done better had it not been staged at the cavernous Broadway Theatre; despite positive reviews and steady attendance, *The New Yorkers* could not make up for the huge expenses and closed after only three months. No doubt, the worsening Depression also had a negative impact on the show's longevity.

"Take Me Back to Manhattan" is one of two love sonnets to New York that Porter wrote for the show. Written during the show's tryouts in Philadelphia, it consists of only one verse and one refrain, but its simplicity sums up his love for "that dear old dirty town." Introduced by actress Frances Williams, the song replaced the first version of "Just One of Those Things."

I Happen to Like New York

During the second week of the run of *The New Yorkers*, Porter sailed away on a vacation to Monte Carlo. Two days out to sea, he wrote "I Happen to Like New York," which he wired to producer E. Ray Goetz. It first appeared in the show during the week of January 19, 1931, sung by Oscar Ragland as a comic hood named Mildew. Taken out of context, the song is more wistful and passionate than "Take Me Back to Manhattan," showing an almost aching attachment to the city. Porter's lyrics are simple, direct, and uncluttered with his usual cultural references and clever rhymes:

I like the city air, I like to drink of it.
The more I know New York, the more I think of it
I like the sight and sound and even the stink of it.

The Great Indoors

In *The New Yorkers*, actress Frances Williams played Mona Low, who sings "The Great Indoors," a song that is noteworthy for including Williams's name in the lyrics:

I take no chances
Sitting on my Frances
In the great indoors.

Mona's name is a take on "Moanin' Low," a hit song by Libby Holman in the 1929 revue *The Little Show*. A secondary character, Mona is not interested in engaging in any of her friends' outdoor physical activities, which she says only serve to bore and make one perspire. Instead, she is content to lounge about, and sip a cool drink in front of an electric fan.

Where Have You Been?

"Where Have You Been?" is a love song sung by Alice Wentworth (Hope Williams), who has fallen in love with the murderous bootlegger Al Spanish (Charles King). Since the lyrics are not specific to the show or the time period, this Porter song can be considered "timeless." It's a love-at-first-sight number that works as a solo as well as a duet. In 1931, it was recorded for Victor by Fred Waring with vocals by The Three Waring Girls. Waring and his band, The Pennsylvanians, were featured in the original production of *The New Yorkers* and wrote one song for the show.

Love for Sale

One of Cole Porter's most famous songs ignited a scandal of epic proportions when it made its debut in *The New Yorkers*. "Love for Sale" is sung by May (Kathryn Crawford), a lonely prostitute, in front of a popular midtown restaurant. The song is one of aching sympathy for the desolate, loveless life of the street walker. Critics erupted with cries of protest, saying that the sequence is "in the worst possible taste," and the producers caved in to the criticism. After one performance, they replaced Crawford with African-American Elisabeth Welch and moved the setting uptown to Harlem's Cotton Club. (During those times, it was considered more appropriate for a black person, rather than a white person, to portray such a disreputable character.) Libby Holman's Brunswick recording became the first of many versions to become popular, despite the fact that recordings of "Love for Sale" were later banned from radio airplay. The song became one of Porter's best-known numbers, and was the composer's personal favorite of all the songs he wrote.

I've Got You on My Mind

Porter initially wrote "I've Got You on My Mind" for *The New Yorkers*, but it was targeted for a new Cole Porter musical called *Star Dust*. According to Porter, the musical was never produced because a large tobacco company that had agreed to provide the seed money backed out of the production when a tax was added to the sale of cigarettes. "I've Got You on My Mind" eventually emerged in Porter's next show, *Gay Divorce* (1932), which starred Fred Astaire. The song is a musical conversation sung by Guy Holden (Astaire), an American writer, and Mimi Pratt (Claire Luce), a young lady with whom he has fallen in love.

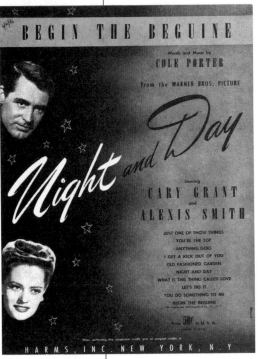

Sheet music from the 1946 film biography of Cole Porter, *Night and Day*, starring Cary Grant as Porter.

Night and Day

Cole Porter's most famous song, "Night and Day," is sung by the character of Guy Holden (Fred Astaire) to Mimi Pratt (Claire Luce) in *Gay Divorce*, followed by an elegant dance. Porter was fond of claiming this song was inspired by a Mohammedan call to worship he had heard in Morocco. The song was written specifically with Astaire's limited vocal range in mind. In the verse, Porter uses a deliberately monotonous melody (consisting of only three notes) and repeated use of the words "beat," "drip," "tick," and "you" to represent the singer's obsession. The song became hugely popular, overriding the success of the show itself. In fact, to Broadway-goers, the musical was more familiarly known as "The Night and Day Show." Porter was especially proud of a letter he received from Irving Berlin, who called "Night and Day" the best tune of the year. During the show's run, Leo Reisman and His Orchestra made an extremely popular recording of the song for Brunswick Records, featuring a vocal by Astaire. Another popular version came in 1942 when the Tommy Dorsey Orchestra recorded it, featuring a vocal by a young Frank Sinatra. *Night and Day* is also the title of Porter's 1946 film biography.

Mister and Missus Fitch

Cole Porter loved practical jokes and pranks, especially when it involved his friends as targets or co-conspirators. While writing songs for *Star Dust*, he concocted a fictional social-climbing couple that he called Mr. and Mrs. S. Beech Fitch. With the help of professional hostess / gossip columnist Elsa Maxwell and some other friends, Porter sent letters to the *New York Herald Tribune* that purportedly came from the imaginary couple from Tulsa, Oklahoma. After Porter killed off the Fitches in an auto accident, the hoax was exposed by columnists Walter Winchell and Maury Paul (a.k.a "Cholly Knickerbocker"). The Fitches were immortalized in "Mister and Missus Fitch," which was eventually incorporated into *Gay Divorce*. Introduced by Luella Gear, the song features the words "son of a bitch" in the lyrics. Those words are meant to be sung, but they were drowned out by the pit orchestra's drummer.

After You, Who?

In a 1953 letter, Cole Porter revealed that Fred Astaire had agreed to appear in *Gay Divorce* after hearing Porter play "After You, Who?" for him. This was Astaire's last appearance on Broadway. After the show closed, the famed actor/dancer left the stage forever for an even more successful career in motion pictures. The lyrics represent both the rapture of being in love and the anxiety of what it would be like if the love ended.

How's Your Romance?

Character actor Erik Rhodes, who played Rodolfo Tonetti in *Gay Divorce*, sang the delightful "How's Your Romance." The song reflects Cole Porter's love for Italy, where he had spent many summers. The attention lavished on "Night and Day" tended to obscure the value of "How's Your Romance" as well as other songs in *Gay Divorce*. Rhodes also sings the tune in the 1934 film version, also starring Fred Astaire. The production's title was changed to *The Gay Divorcée*, under the assumption that nobody enjoys a divorce, but a divorcée could indeed enjoy playing the field.

Experiment

Nymph Errant is based on a book by James Laver that tells of the amorous exploits of a young English girl. Fresh from a Swiss finishing school, she is ready to take on the world, one suitor at a time. The show had a tryout in Manchester, England, before proceeding to London, where it opened to a glittering audience of British high society on October 6, 1933. It starred Gertrude Lawrence in the lead role of Evangeline Edwards and featured choreographer Agnes de Mille in her first major assignment. Beset by a variety of issues

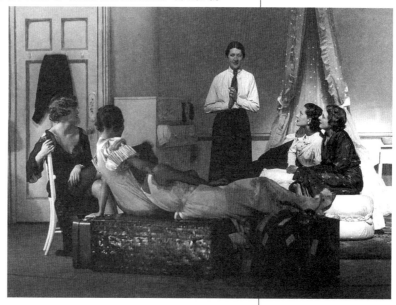

Miss Pratt (Moya Nugent) sings "Experiment" to her finishing school students in *Nymph Errant* (1933).

that prevented it from crossing the Atlantic to Broadway—including the illness of its star, a story that is disagreeable to moralists, and the fact that it has no central male romantic lead—*Nymph Errant* played 154 performances in London but was not staged in the U.S. for almost 50 years after its opening. Despite the show's lackluster track record, its score was Porter's personal favorite. "Experiment" embodies much of Porter's attitude in life and the theatre and is sung by Evangeline's finishing school teacher, Miss Pratt (Moya Nugent), before the impressionable girl is turned loose on the world. Although Miss Pratt advises Evangeline to shun convention and try new experiences, Evangeline takes the advice in a very different way and proceeds to romance and discard a culturally diverse succession of men.

It's Bad for Me

In *Nymph Errant*, Evangeline (Gertrude Lawrence) realizes the power of her femininity as she revels in a suitor's obsession over her. Porter's lyrics deftly traverse back and forth between Evangeline's amazement that anyone would feel this way for her and her belief that returning his affection would be harmful to her. The playful, witty song was revived in a 1955 recording by Rosemary Clooney with the Benny Goodman Sextet.

How Could We Be Wrong?

This love-at-first-sight song from *Nymph Errant* shows Cole Porter at his most romantic. Despite setback after setback, Evangeline continues to hope that her next love will be the one to last. Porter's lyrics are simple, direct, and eloquent. The genius of Cole Porter lays in his ability to be sophisticated and erudite in his list songs, yet passionate and idealistic in his love songs.

The Physician

A song that did not survive the Broadway tryouts for *The New Yorkers* became the hit of *Nymph Errant* three years later. Originally called "But He Never Says He Loves Me," the song's title was changed to "The Physician" during rehearsals for *Nymph Errant*. Sung by Evangeline, the song concerns her love for a doctor

Gertrude Lawrence in *Nymph Errant*.

who doesn't return her affections, but, instead, admires her anatomy in gleefully scientific detail. The wickedly clever way Porter incorporates the multi-syllabic medical terms into his lyrics gives the song its air of bawdiness, as in this couplet:

He murmured "Molto bella"
When I sat on his patella.

I Get a Kick Out of You

Cole Porter called *Anything Goes* the most famous show he was associated with. The show starred the iridescent Ethel Merman as nightclub singer Reno Sweeney with the team of William Gaxton and Victor Moore. Of Merman, Porter told the *New York Times*, "She has the finest enunciation of any American singer I know." In turn, Merman complimented Porter by saying, "I'd rather sing his songs than those by any other writer." The combination of Porter's songs and Merman's voice was the highlight of *Anything Goes*, a knockabout comedy about love and mistaken identity aboard a luxury cruise liner. The show was not only the biggest hit of the 1934–35 season, but the quintessential musical comedy of the 1930s. It is filled with raucous slapstick, leggy chorus girls, comical villains, and, above all, Cole Porter's sophisticated, brilliant songs. In Merman's opening number, "I Get a Kick Out of You," she lingered on the second syllable of the word "terrif-ically," virtually splitting the word in two. Merman recalled that Porter loved her phrasing of the word. The song was originally scheduled for the unproduced musical *Star Dust*.

All Through the Night

In *Anything Goes*, William Gaxton, who played the romantic lead role of Billy Crocker, was slated to sing Porter's "Easy to Love" to the character of debutante Hope Harcourt, played by Bettina Hall. When Gaxton couldn't handle the high notes in the song, Porter replaced it with "All Through the Night," a spellbinding and sensuous love song with an unusually long, 64-measure Latin-flavored melody. Most of the song's melody lines are chromatic, which gives it its singularly hypnotic quality. In the 1987 revival, it was moved to Act II and "Easy to Love" was returned to its original place in the score.

You're the Top

The quintessential Cole Porter list song "You're the Top" is sung by Reno Sweeney (Ethel Merman) and Billy Crocker (William Gaxton). It is a playfully romantic number, which allowed Porter to contribute a virtually endless list of cleverly juxtaposed pop cultural references into its rhyming scheme. Porter wrote the song in Paris while dining with Mrs. Alistair Mackintosh as they entertained themselves by seeing how many rhymed superlatives they could come up with. The song became so popular that New York newspapers reported that writing new verses for the song had become a favorite game around town. At the peak of this trend, a reported 300 parodies per month were being sent to Porter. None other than Irving Berlin, himself, wrote a scatological version, which Porter delighted in singing. Merman later said that Porter had invented a completely original kind of love song. The composer recorded the song for Victor in 1934, accompanying himself on the piano.

William Gaxton and Ethel Merman singing "You're the Top" from *Anything Goes*.

Anything Goes

The title song for *Anything Goes* is the perfect combination of melodic and lyric mastery. Its sprightly, syncopated tune is matched by its witty, sly references to cultural icons like President and Mrs. Roosevelt, actress Mae West, film mogul Samuel Goldwyn, and theater producer Max Gordon. The lyrics celebrate the permissive habits of the well-to-do, mentioning such risqué topics as nudist parties and novels with four-letter words. Reno Sweeney (Ethel Merman) sings the song at the end of the show's first act, which brought down the curtain to tumultuous cheers and applause.

Blow, Gabriel, Blow

During the late 1920s and early 1930s, Tin Pan Alley became infatuated with rhythmic spirituals—high-spirited songs patterned after those sung at southern revival meetings. This trend resulted in the popularity of jazzy numbers like Sam Coslow and Frank Harling's "Sing You Sinners," Jimmie Lunceford's "In Dat Mornin'," and Andy Razaf's "On Revival Day." The mock-sermonizing on these and other records fascinated Cole Porter, who made his contribution to this idea with "Blow, Gabriel, Blow." This show-stopping number from *Anything Goes* is delivered with brassy gusto by former evangelist Reno Sweeney

(Ethel Merman). Even though Merman was already a star, thanks to her Broadway debut in *Girl Crazy* (1930), her work in *Anything Goes* cemented her fame as the most popular Broadway performer of the 1930s. As a result of the powerhouse songs Porter wrote for her, the two developed a lifelong friendship. Merman starred in four subsequent Porter musicals.

Buddie, Beware

"Buddie, Beware," an "11 o'clock number" sung by Ethel Merman, was dropped from *Anything Goes* shortly after the show's New York debut and replaced by a reprise of "I Get a Kick Out of You." It was restored, however, for the 1987 Broadway revival. In this comic song, Reno Sweeney (Merman) warns potential suitors that she is extremely high maintenance and requires things that other women would consider luxuries, such as Rolls Royces, caviar, and expensive jewelry from Cartier's.

Ethel Merman and chorus girls sing "Buddie, Beware."

Miss Otis Regrets

One of Porter's greatest cabaret songs, "Miss Otis Regrets" was originally scheduled to appear in an unproduced musical called *Ever Yours*, which was a collaboration between Porter and British playwright Guy Bolton. The song finally emerged in the 1934 London production of *Hi Diddle Diddle*, in which it was sung by bawdy British comic Douglas Byng. Written in the style of American folk murder ballads such as "Frankie and Johnny," it concerns a "woman gone wrong" who shoots a lover that deserted her. At the conclusion of the narrative, she is sent to the gallows, but not before delivering the understated message, "Miss Otis regrets she's unable to lunch today." Porter never revealed who Miss Otis was, if she even existed, but he once claimed to have happened upon the name "Otis" accidentally, while thumbing through a copy of the Social Register.

Why Shouldn't I?

Between January and May 1935, Cole Porter embarked on a world cruise with director Moss Hart. During the cruise, Porter wrote the torch song "Why Shouldn't I?" which was used in the show *Jubilee*. The song is about longing for a love that has not yet happened. Beautifully crafted and restrained, it was introduced by Margaret Adams, who played the role of Princess Diana. A recently discovered interlude reveals the target of the character's affection: playwright/composer/actor Eric Dare (Derek Williams). "Why Shouldn't I?" eventually became a standard, but was overshadowed by "Just One of Those Things" and "Begin the Beguine."

Porter and friends onboard the *Franconia* as they pass through the Panama Canal during a world cruise, 1935. From left to right: travel writer William Powell, Howard Sturges, Linda Porter, Monty Woolley, Porter, and director Moss Hart.

Just One of Those Things

Although many of the songs from *Jubilee* were composed during Porter's 1935 world cruise, "Just One of Those Things" wasn't written until August, more than two months after he had returned to the U.S. By this time, auditions were being conducted, and Moss Hart and Porter were relaxing at the Ohio farm of Leonard Hanna, one of Porter's old Yale classmates. Hart asked Porter to write another song for Act II, and Porter responded by delivering "Just One of Those Things" the very next day. The song is a so-called "11 o'clock number," introduced in *Jubilee* by June Knight and Charles Walters, but by the time it was performed some critics had already departed the theatre and never got a chance to hear it. Its widespread success did not come until the 1940s, when it became a favorite of jazz musicians Sidney Bechet and Art Tatum. "Just One of Those Things" is different from another song with the same title that was removed from *The New Yorkers* in 1930.

Begin the Beguine

The song from *Jubilee* that receives the most acclaim is "Begin the Beguine," which became one of Cole Porter's best-loved hits. The true origins of the song are unclear; a contributing factor to this is Porter's own contradictory versions of when and how he wrote it. As one story goes, Porter was living in Paris in 1925 when he went to see a performance by the Black Martiniquois tribe. The Martiniquois performed a native dance they called "The Beguine," which Porter described as a faster version of the rhumba. He thought up the song title first and filed it away in a notebook, along with jottings concerning the song's rhythm and tempo. Ten years later, while on his world cruise with Moss Hart, Porter came across a similar-sounding dance that was native to an island west of New Guinea in the Lesser Sunda chain. After hearing the first four bars of the song, Porter recalled the song title he had written down 10 years earlier: "Begin the Beguine." He then wrote the exotic-sounding song that consists of a melody from the South Pacific with a Caribbean rhythm.

The structure of "Begin the Beguine" was revolutionary for its time. Porter abandoned the traditional 32-bar Tin Pan Alley verse/chorus pattern in favor of one with no verse, no release, and an uninterrupted chorus that lasts 108 measures. In 1972, musicologist Alec Wilder pronounced it the longest popular song ever written. It is also one of the most difficult Cole Porter songs for vocalists. The first hit recording was a 1935 version by Xavier Cugat and His Waldorf Astoria Orchestra. The song didn't take off until 1938, when a swing instrumental version by Artie Shaw and His Orchestra became a multi-million seller and the biggest hit of Shaw's career. As a result, "Begin the Beguine" was incorporated into the film musical *Broadway Melody of 1940*; it is sung operatic style by Lois Hodnott, then in swing style by The Music Maids, followed by a lengthy tap dance sequence by Fred Astaire and Eleanor Powell.

June Knight, who sang "Begin the Beguine" in *Jubilee* (1935).

Easy to Love

In 1936, Cole Porter "went Hollywood" and began a regular pattern of working on one film musical and one Broadway show every year during the 1930s and '40s. *Born to Dance* stars James Stewart and Eleanor Powell in a conventional boy-meets-girl love story with plenty of opportunities for Powell to display her tap-dancing talents. The movie features eight Porter compositions, including "Easy to Love," which was originally intended for William Gaxton in *Anything Goes*. In *Born to Dance*, it is sung by sailor Ted Barker (Stewart) and lonely-hearts club hostess Nora Paige (Powell, whose singing voice was dubbed by Marjorie Lane). Of Stewart's thin, untrained vocal, Porter wrote, "He sings far from well, although he has nice notes in his voice." But Stewart was able to sell the song through his charming, affable performance. The couplet "So sweet to waken with / So nice to sit down to eggs and bacon with" was censored due to its implication that the characters had slept together. Porter replaced it with a more discreetly worded lyric.

James Stewart sings "Easy to Love" with Eleanor Powell in *Born to Dance* (1936).

I've Got You Under My Skin

Like "Begin the Beguine," "I've Got You Under My Skin" has an unconventional musical structure: seven eight-measure phrases, each different from the another. Unlike "Easy to Love," it is sung in *Born to Dance* by a superb vocalist, actress Virginia Bruce. It became the biggest hit of the movie and one of Porter's most popular standards. The song later became a staple in the repertoire of Frank Sinatra, among others.

Ours

Red, Hot and Blue! had a wacky plot about a national lottery conducted to find a girl who had sat on a waffle iron when she was four. It features the song "Ours," a Porter comic-romantic duet that refers to a variety of Manhattan hot spots. The song is introduced by secondary characters Anne Westcott (Dorothy Vernon) and Sonny Hadley (Thurston Crane). *Red, Hot and Blue!* was slated to star leading man William Gaxton and the incendiary Ethel Merman. Gaxton withdrew, however, fearing that Merman would outshine him on stage, and Bob Hope replaced him. When an argument over billing developed between Merman and co-star Jimmy Durante, Linda Porter devised the solution to feature a criss-crossed billing design above the show's title, in which the positions of the names would be switched every few weeks.

Playbill for *Red, Hot and Blue!*, featuring Jimmy Durante, Ethel Merman, and Bob Hope.

Down in the Depths (On the 90th Floor)

One of Ethel Merman's rare torch songs from *Red, Hot and Blue!* became a hit of the show. Porter had been asked to replace the song "Goodbye, Little Dream, Goodbye" with something less somber and, two days later, he delivered "Down in the Depths (On the 90th Floor)." Despondent manicurist "Nails" Duquesne (Merman) sings this one while looking out the window of her opulently furnished Manhattan penthouse apartment. Porter, touched by Merman's uncharacteristically understated performance of the song, later reflected, "One thinks of these things on the morning after an opening, with affection and gratitude. For, after all is said and done, a songwriter is very much at the mercy of his interpreters."

It's De-Lovely

The highlight of *Red, Hot and Blue!* is "It's De-Lovely," a "de-lightful, de-licious, and de-lectable" musical dialog between Bob Hale (Bob Hope) and Nails Duquesne (Ethel Merman). The song traces the characters' relationship from their first kiss to their firstborn, with a catchy melody amplified by variations on the word "de-lovely." Porter builds upon this with a barrage of other words beginning with the same first syllable.

Bob Hope and Ethel Merman during a performance of "It's De-Lovely."

Ridin' High

Another song from *Red, Hot and Blue!* is more typical of the kind Ethel Merman is best known for singing. "Ridin' High" has the brassy optimism Merman showcased later in songs like "Everything's Coming Up Roses" from *Gypsy*. Nails Duquesne (Merman) has just discovered that Bob Hale (Bob Hope) is in love with her. Her euphoria is so complete that, in two patter sections (where words are sung quickly), she rates herself superior to the reigning prominent females of the day. She goes on to note the most readily identifiable attribute of each—including Katharine Hepburn's nose, Marlene Dietrich's legs, Barbara Hutton's wealth, and Dorothy Parker's wit.

Goodbye, Little Dream, Goodbye

Although "Goodbye, Little Dream, Goodbye" had been replaced by other songs in two prior musicals, it was finally included in the 1936 London production of *O Mistress Mine*, sung by Yvonne Printemps. The number has since enjoyed a renaissance as one of Cole Porter's best-loved torch songs. Producer Sam Katz noted its particularly Jewish-sounding melody, a concept that Porter consciously cultivated in songs such as "Night and Day," "Begin the Beguine," and "Love for Sale."

The Cole Porter Song Collection (Volume Two)

The second volume of *The Cole Porter Song Collection* features songs from the latter period of Porter's career (1937–1958). Although Porter suffered greatly from the effects of a debilitating riding accident in 1937, his later years produced some of his best-loved work. These later songs were featured in Broadway musicals such as *Kiss Me, Kate* and *Can-Can* and motion pictures including *High Society* and *Silk Stockings*.

Cary Ginell

Popular Music Editor
Alfred Music Publishing Co., Inc.

Cole Porter in Hollywood, 1936.

Dorothie Bigelow, in *See America First*, 1916. Bigelow was Porter's first leading lady.

An early Yale football song, with lyrics by Porter, 1911.

Sheet music for a song from *Hitchy-Koo of 1919*.

Columbia recording by Charles Adams Prince's Orchestra of "Old-Fashioned Garden," Porter's first big hit.

William Gaxton
and Genevieve Tobin,
stars of *Fifty Million
Frenchmen* (1929).

Cole Porter relaxes on
the Lido in Venice, 1923.

Gertrude Lawrence sang "They All Fall in Love"
in Paramount's *The Battle of Paris*, the first
movie to feature songs by Cole Porter.

Gertrude Lawrence in *Nymph Errant*, 1933.

Porter with Amelia Earhart, c. 1935.

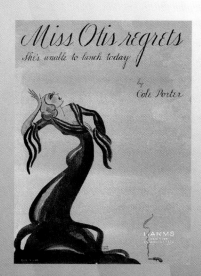

A rare recording of Cole Porter singing and playing his own composition, "You're the Top," for Victor Records, 1934.

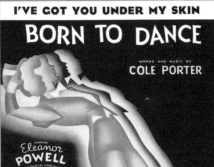

Virginia Bruce sings "I've Got You Under My Skin" to James Stewart in *Born to Dance* (1936).

Chorus line from *Anything Goes* (1934).

Sheet music from the film version of *Anything Goes* (1936).

ANYTHING GOES

(from the 1987 Revival *Anything Goes*)

Words and Music by
COLE PORTER

*Reno's solo has been excerpted from the complete show version of the song.
**Fb = E

Anything Goes - 11 - 1
33309

28

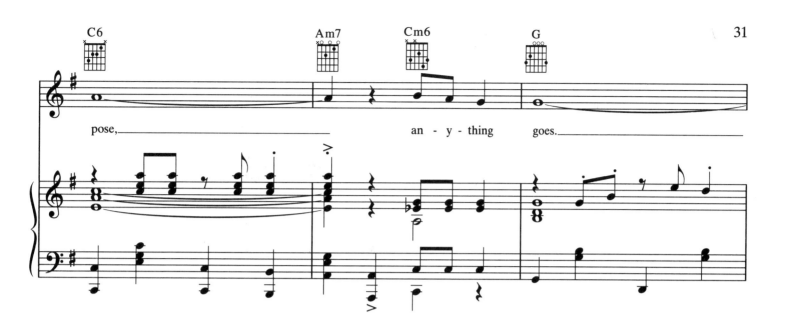

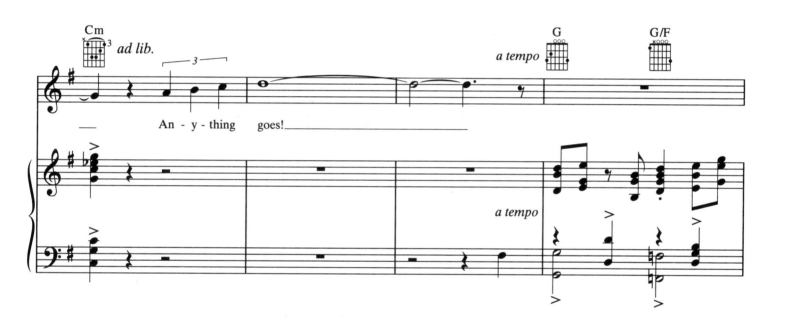

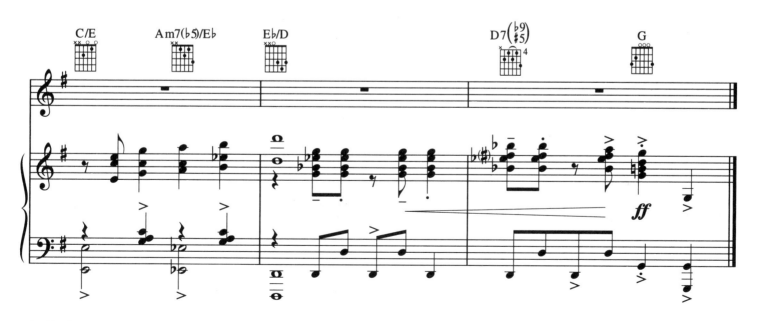

AFTER YOU, WHO?

(from *Gay Divorce*)

Words and Music by
COLE PORTER

ALL THROUGH THE NIGHT

(from *Anything Goes*)

Words and Music by
COLE PORTER

Moderately

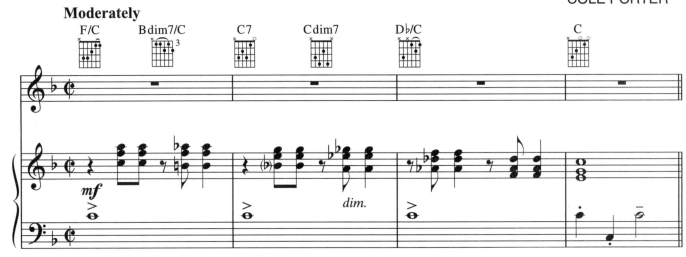

Verse:

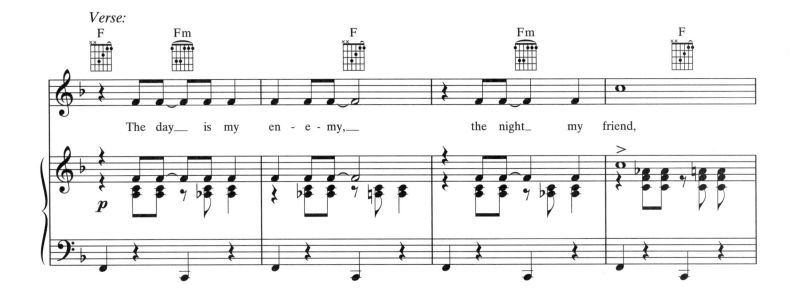

The day__ is my en-e-my,__ the night__ my friend,

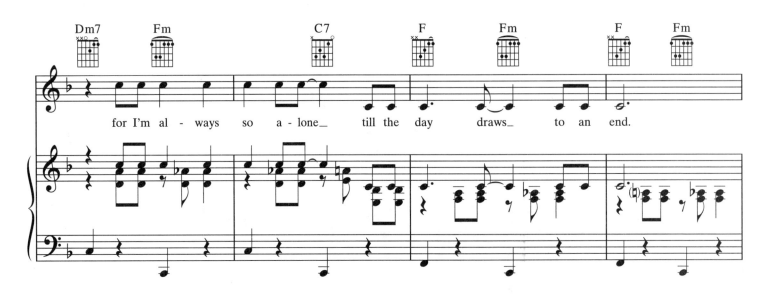

for I'm al-ways so a-lone__ till the day draws__ to an end.

BEGIN THE BEGUINE
(from *Jubilee* and *Broadway Melody of 1940*)

Words and Music by
COLE PORTER

know but too well what they mean. So don't

let them be - gin the be - guine, let the

love that was once a fire re-main an em - ber. Let it

sleep like the dead de - sire I on-ly re-mem - ber

BLOW, GABRIEL, BLOW

(from *Anything Goes*)

Words and Music by
COLE PORTER

Poco agitato

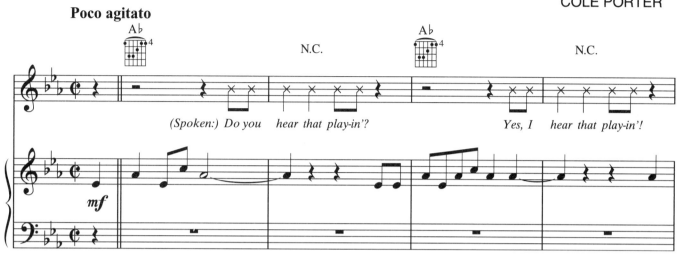

(Spoken:) Do you hear that play-in'? Yes, I hear that play-in'!

Do you know who's play-in'? No, who is that play-in'? Why, it's *(Sung:)*

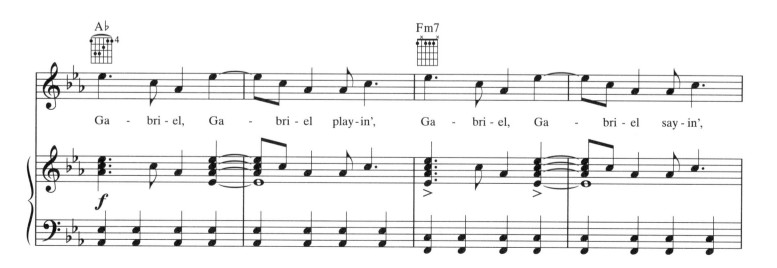

Ga - bri - el, Ga - bri - el play-in', Ga - bri - el, Ga - bri - el say-in',

50

BUDDIE, BEWARE

(from *Anything Goes*)

Words and Music by
COLE PORTER

Andante (very slow)

Refrain:

Refrain 2:
Buddie, beware.
Buddie, better take care.
Even angels, I'm told,
Are still harping on gold,
So, buddie, beware,
Somehow I don't feel nice
When I wear a dress twice.
Since the day I was weaned,
I'm a caviar fiend,
So, buddie, beware.
Now and then I like to see
Willie Stewart and Company
'Cause I hear divine voices
When their Rolls-Royces
Come and honk for me.
But if you insist
And we riddle love's mysteries,
I would hate leaving you
For Wooley Donahue,
But, buddie, beware.

Refrain 3:
Buddie, beware.
Buddie, better take care.
I must warn you that I'm
Simply never on time,
So, buddie, beware.
When you order a steak
And no supper I'll take.
If you tell me I'm rude
When I play with your food,
Then, buddie, beware.
I feel I should put you right.
As I lie in bed at night
While the twinkling stars gleam on,
With my cold cream on
I'm a lovely sight.
And another thing, too,
When I'm married to you, my sweet,
If to come home you fail,
I'll open all your mail,
So, buddie, beware.

DON'T LOOK AT ME THAT WAY

(from *Paris*)

Words and Music by
COLE PORTER

DOWN IN THE DEPTHS
(ON THE 90TH FLOOR)

(from *Red, Hot and Blue!*)

Words and Music by
COLE PORTER

Refrain: (strict slow fox-trot tempo)

EASY TO LOVE

(from *Born to Dance*)

Words and Music by
COLE PORTER

(*Slowly, with much expression*)
Refrain:

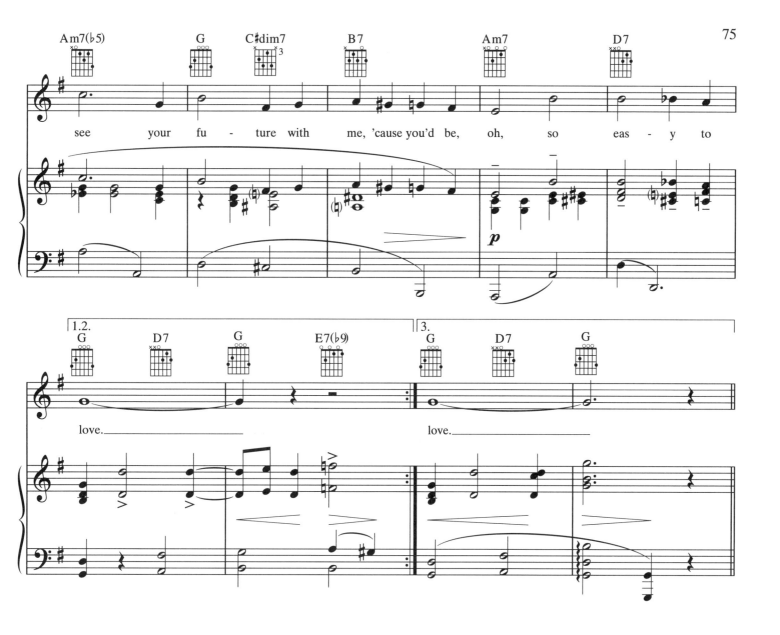

see your fu - ture with me, 'cause you'd be, oh, so eas - y to

love. _____

love. _____

Refrain 2:
You'd be so easy to love,
So easy to idolize, all others above,
So worth the yearning for,
So swell to keep ev'ry home fire burning for.
Oh, how we'd bloom, how we'd thrive
In a cottage for two, or even three, four, or five,
So try to see
Your future with me,
'Cause they'd be, oh, so easy to love.

Refrain 3:
You'd be so easy to love,
So easy to worship as an angel above,
Just made to pray before,
Just right to stay home and walk the baby for.
I know I once left you cold,
But call me your "lamb" and take me back to the fold.
If you'll agree,
Why, I guarantee
That I'll be, oh, so easy to love.

EXPERIMENT
(from *Nymph Errant*)

Words and Music by
COLE PORTER

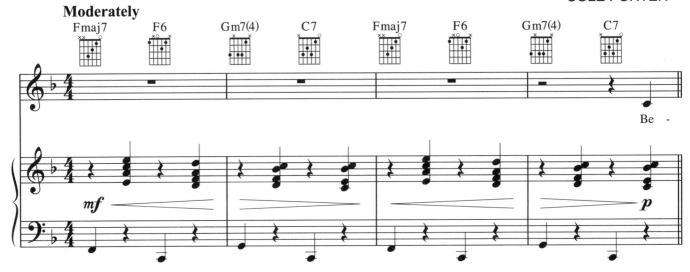

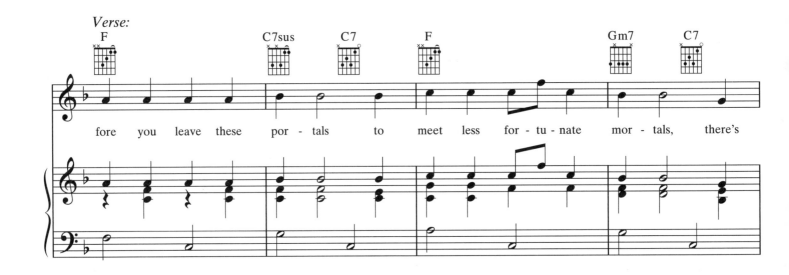

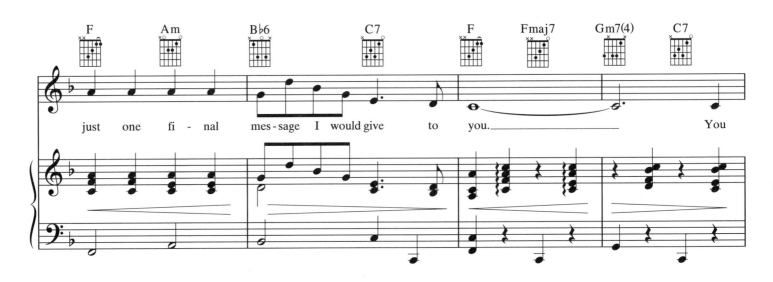

Refrain:

per - i - ment, _____ make it your mot - to day and night. Ex -

per - i - ment, _____ and it will lead you to the light. The

ap - ple on the top of the tree ___ is nev - er too high ___ to a - chieve, so

take an ex - am - ple from Eve, _____ ex - per - i - ment. _____ Be

GOODBYE, LITTLE DREAM, GOODBYE

(from *O Mistress Mine*)

Words and Music by
COLE PORTER

THE GREAT INDOORS

(from *The New Yorkers*)

Words and Music by
COLE PORTER

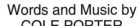

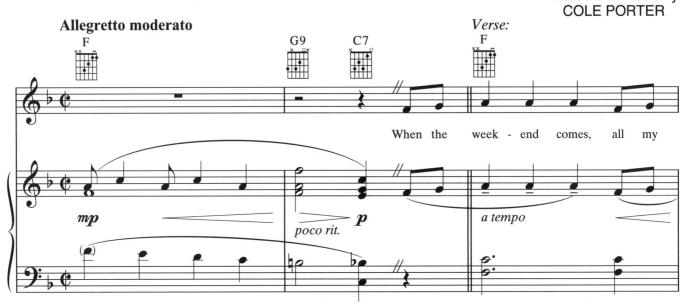

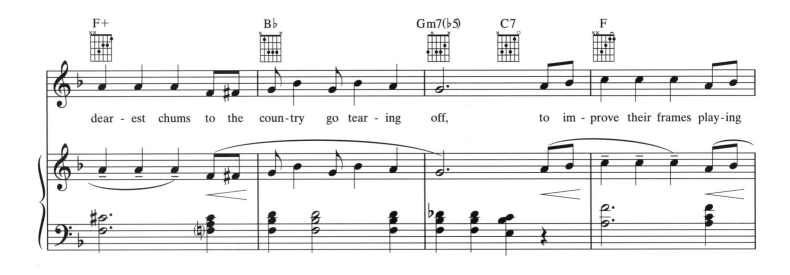

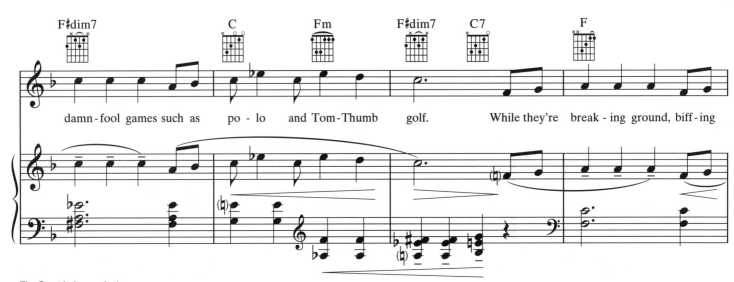

When the week-end comes, all my dear-est chums to the coun-try go tear-ing off, to im-prove their frames play-ing damn-fool games such as po-lo and Tom-Thumb golf. While they're break-ing ground, biff-ing

The Great Indoors - 4 - 1
33309

HOW COULD WE BE WRONG?
(from *Nymph Errant*)

Words and Music by
COLE PORTER

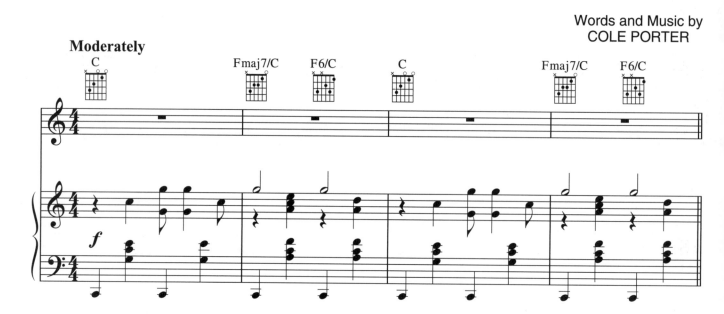

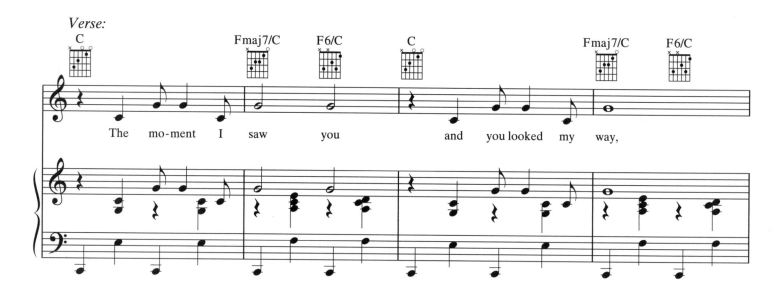

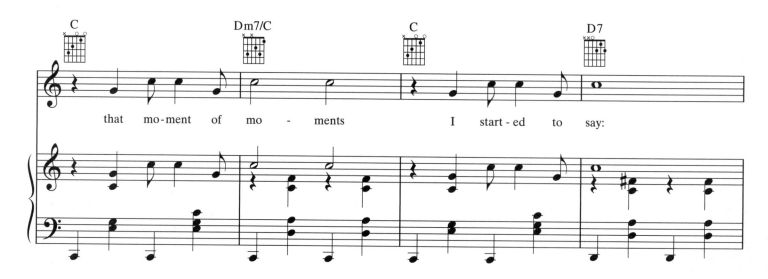

HOW'S YOUR ROMANCE?

(from *Gay Divorce*)

Words and Music by
COLE PORTER

Verse:

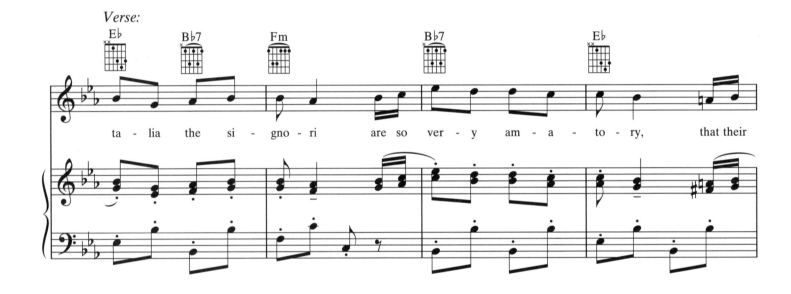

ta - lia the si - gno - ri are so ver - y am - a - to - ry, that their

pas - sion, a pri - or - i, is l'a - mor'. Is it al - ways l'a - mor'? Si,

How's Your Romance - 6 - 1
33309

94

I GET A KICK OUT OF YOU

(from *Anything Goes*)

Words and Music by
COLE PORTER

I HAPPEN TO LIKE NEW YORK

(from *The New Yorkers*)

Words and Music by
COLE PORTER

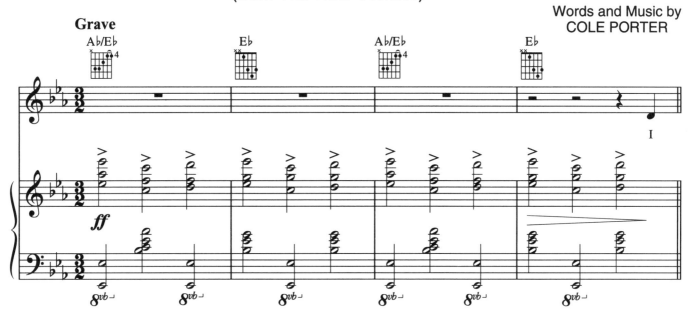

I'M IN LOVE AGAIN

(from *Greenwich Village Follies of 1924*)

Words and Music by
COLE PORTER

Lyrics:

1. Why am I just as hap-py as a child?___
2. Some-one sad had the aw-ful luck to meet___

Why am I like a race-horse run-ning wild?___
some-one bad, but the kind of bad that's sweet.___

I'M UNLUCKY AT GAMBLING

(from *Fifty Million Frenchmen*)

Words and Music by
COLE PORTER

Refrain:

IT'S BAD FOR ME

(from *Nymph Errant*)

Words and Music by
COLE PORTER

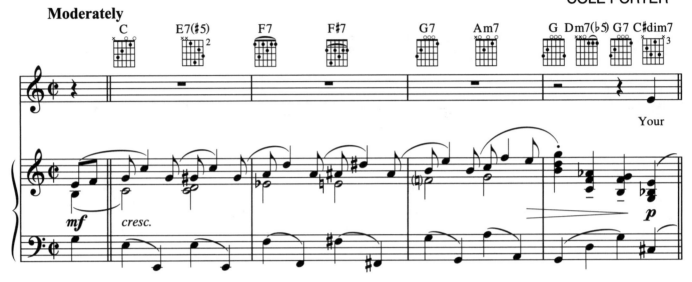

Verse:

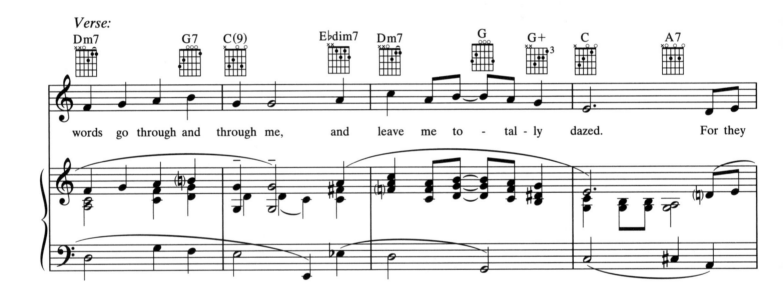

words go through and through me, and leave me to - tal - ly dazed. For they

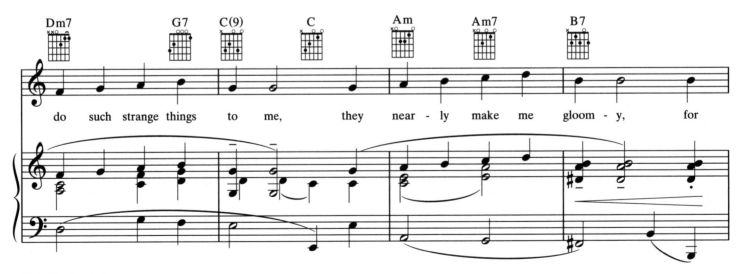

do such strange things to me, they near - ly make me gloom - y, for

It's Bad for Me - 4 - 1
33309

IT'S DE-LOVELY
(from *Red, Hot and Blue!*)

Words and Music by
COLE PORTER

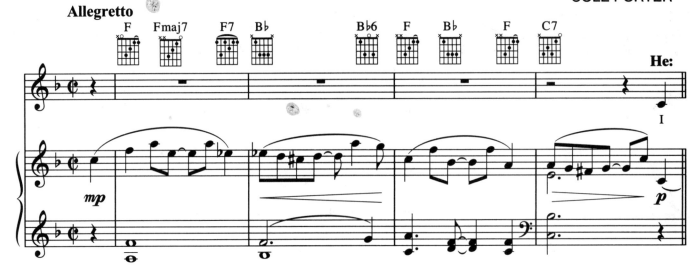

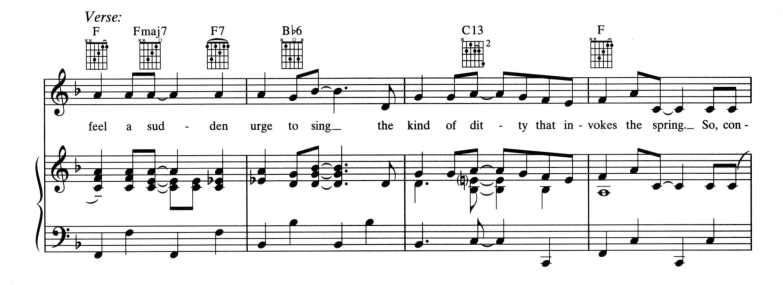

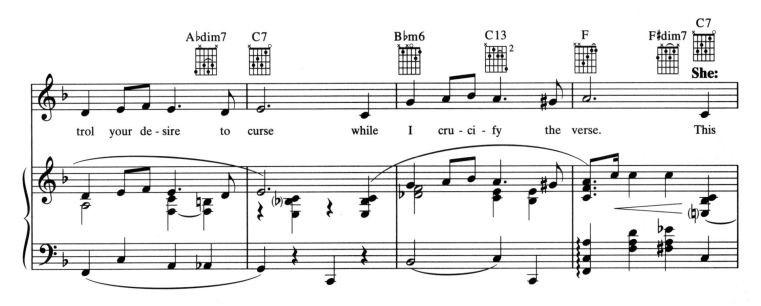

It's De-Lovely - 6 - 1
33309

Very rhythmically

Refrain:

night is young, the skies are clear, so if you want to go

walk - ing, dear, it's de - light - ful, it's de - li - cious, it's de -

love - ly. I un - der - stand the rea - son why you're

sen - ti - men - tal, 'cause so am I. It's de - light - ful, it's de -

* Pronounced "delukes."

Verse 2:

She: Oh, charming sir, the way you sing
Would break the heart of Missus Crosby's Bing,
For the tone of your tra la la
Has that certain je ne sais quoi.

He: Oh, thank thee kindly, winsome wench,
But 'stead of falling into Berlitz French
Just warble to me, please,
This beautiful strain in plain Brooklynese.

She: Mi, mi, mi, mi,
Re, re, re, re,
Do, sol, mi, do, la, si.

He: *Take it away.*

Refrain 2:

Time marches on and soon it's plain
You've won my heart and I've lost my brain,
It's delightful, it's delicious, it's de-lovely.
Life seems so sweet that we decide
It's in the bag to get unified,
It's delightful, it's delicious, it's de-lovely.
See the crowd in the church,
See the proud parson plopped up on his perch,
Get the sweet beat of that organ, sealing our doom,
"Here goes the groom, boom!"
How they cheer and how they smile
As we go galloping down that aisle.
"It's divine, dear, it's diveen, dear,
It's de-wunderbar, it's de-victory,
It's de-vallop, it's de-vinner, it's de-voiks,
It's de-lovely."

Refrain 3:

The knot is tied and so we take
A few hours off to eat wedding cake,
It's delightful, it's delicious, it's de-lovely.
It feels so fine to be a bride,
And how's the groom? Why, he's slightly fried,
It's delightful, it's delicious, it's de-lovely.
To the pop of champagne,
Off we hop in our plush little plane
Till a bright light through the darkness cozily calls,
"Niag'ra Falls."
All's well, my love, our day's complete,
And what a beautiful bridal suite,
"It's de-reamy, it's de-rowsy,
It's de-reverie, it's de-rhapsody,
It's de-regal, it's de-royal, it's de-Ritz,
It's de-lovely."

Refrain 4:

We settle down as man and wife
To solve the riddle called "married life,"
It's delightful, it's delicious, it's de-lovely.
We're on the crest, we have no cares.
We're just a couple of honey bears,
It's delightful, it's delicious, it's de-lovely.
All's as right as can be
Till, one night, at my window I see
An absurd bird with a bundle hung on his nose–
"Get baby clo'es."
Those eyes of yours are filled with joy
When Nurse appears and cries, "It's a boy,"
"He's appalling, he's appealing,
He's a pollywog, he's a paragon,
He's a Popeye, he's a panic, he's a pip,
He's de-lovely."

Refrain 5:

Our boy grows up, he's six feet three,
He's so good-looking, he looks like me,
It's delightful, it's delicious, it's de-lovely.
He's such a hit, this son of ours,
That all the dowagers send him flowers,
It's delightful, it's delicious, it's de-lovely.
So sublime is his press
That in time, L.B. Mayer, no less,
Makes a night flight to New York and tells him he should
Go Hollywood.
Good God! today, he gets such pay
That Elaine Barrie's his fiancée,
"It's delightful, it's delicious,
It's delectable, it's delirious,
It's dilemma, it's delimit, it's deluxe,
It's de-lovely."

I'VE A SHOOTING BOX IN SCOTLAND

(from *See America First*)

Words and Music by
COLE PORTER

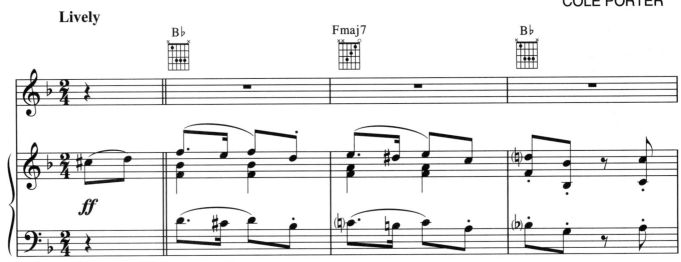

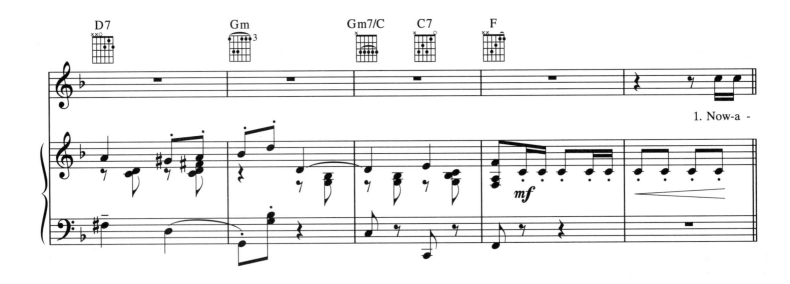

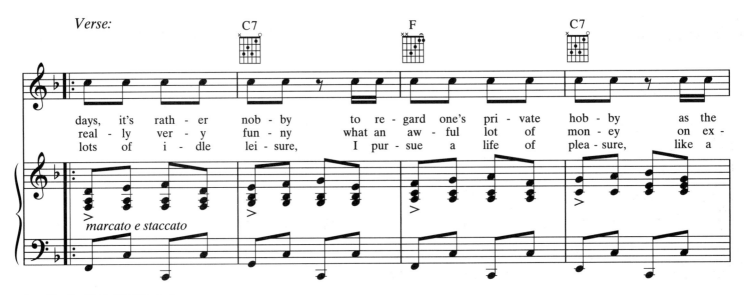

I'VE GOT YOU ON MY MIND

(from *Star Dust* and *Gay Divorce*)

Words and Music by
COLE PORTER

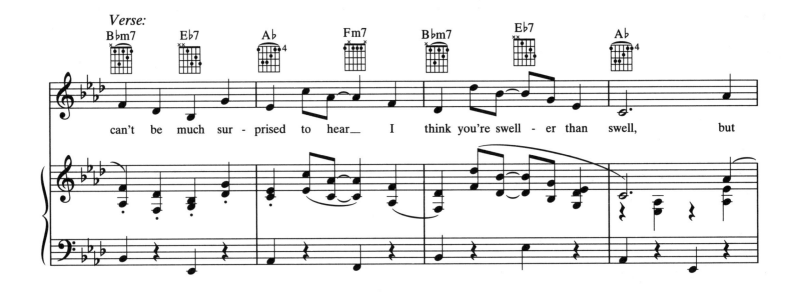

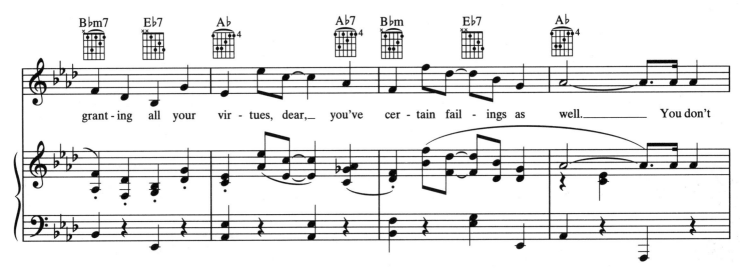

I've Got You on My Mind - 4 - 1
33309

Refrain:

I'VE GOT YOU UNDER MY SKIN

(from *Born to Dance*)

Words and Music by
COLE PORTER

JUST ONE OF THOSE THINGS

(from *Jubilee*)

Words and Music by
COLE PORTER

Just One of Those Things - 6 - 1
33309

THE LAZIEST GAL IN TOWN

(from *Stage Fright*)

Words and Music by
COLE PORTER

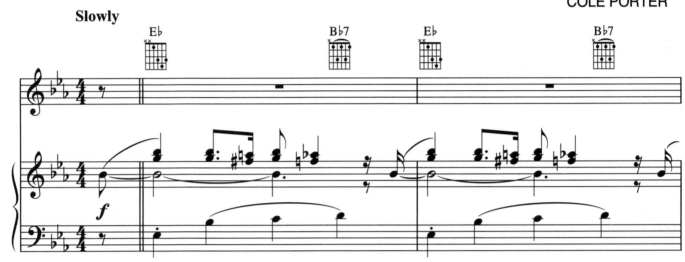

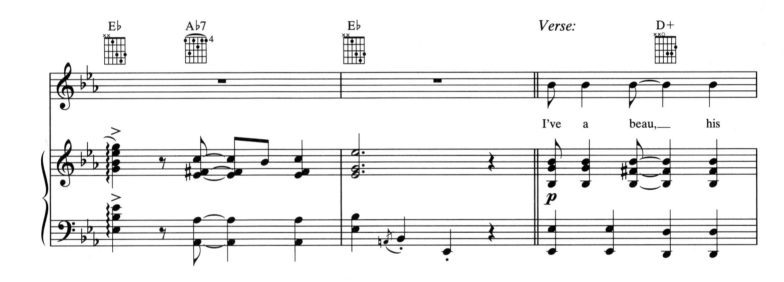

I've a beau,___ his

name is Jim,___ he loves me___ and I love him.___

The Laziest Gal in Town - 5 - 1
33309

148 **Slow and languid**

Refrain:

VERSE SUNG BY MARLENE DIETRICH

Nothing ever worries me,
Nothing ever hurries me.
I take pleasure leisurely
Even when I kiss.
But when I kiss they want some more,
And wanting more becomes a bore,
It isn't worth the fighting for,
So I tell them this:

LET'S DO IT (LET'S FALL IN LOVE)

(from *Paris*)

Words and Music by
COLE PORTER

153

Let's Do It (Let's Fall in Love) - 5 - 3
33309

Original Lyrics (complete)

Verse:
When the little bluebird,
Who has never said a word,
Starts to sing, "Spring, spring,"
When the little bluebell,
In the bottom of the dell,
Starts to ring: "Ding, ding,"
When the little blue clerk,
In the middle of his work,
Starts a tune to the moon up above,
It is nature, that's all,
Simply telling us to fall in love.

Refrain 1:
*And that's why Chinks do it, Japs do it,
Up in Lapland, little Lapps do it,
Let's do it, let's fall in love.
In Spain, the best upper sets do it,
Lithuanians and Letts do it,
Let's do it, let's fall in love.
The Dutch in old Amsterdam do it,
Not to mention the Finns.
Folks in Siam do it;
Think of Siamese twins.
Some Argentines, without means, do it,
People say, in Boston, even beans do it,
Let's do it, let's fall in love.

Refrain 2:
The nightingales, in the dark, do it,
Larks, k-razy for a lark, do it,
Let's do it, let's fall in love.
Canaries, caged in the house, do it,
When they're out of season, grouse do it,
Let's do it, let's fall in love.
The most sedate barnyard fowls do it,
When a chanticleer cries.
High-browed old owls do it,
They're supposed to be wise.
Penguins in flocks, on the rocks, do it,
Even little cuckoos, in their clocks, do it,
Let's do it, let's fall in love.

Refrain 3:
Romantic sponges, they say, do it,
Oysters down in Oyster Bay do it,
Let's do it, let's fall in love.
Cold Cape Cod clams, 'gainst their wish, do it,
Even lazy jellyfish do it,
Let's do it, let's fall in love.
Electric eels, I might add, do it,
Though it shocks 'em, I know.
Why ask if shad do it?
Waiter, bring me shad roe.
In shallow shoals, English soles do it,
Goldfish, in the privacy of bowls, do it,
Let's do it, let's fall in love.

Refrain 3: (English Production)
Young whelks and winkles, in pubs, do it,
Little sponges, in their tubs, do it,
Let's do it, let's fall in love.
Cold salmon, quite 'gainst their wish, do it,
Even lazy jellyfish do it,
Let's do it, let's fall in love.
The most select schools of cod do it,
Though it shocks 'em, I fear.
Sturgeon, thank God, do it,
Have some caviar, dear.
In shady shoals, English soles do it,
Goldfish, in the privacy of bowls, do it,
Let's do it, let's fall in love.

Refrain 4:
The dragonflies, in the reeds, do it,
Sentimental centipedes do it,
Let's do it, let's fall in love.
Mosquitos, heaven forbid, do it,
So does ev'ry katydid do it,
Let's do it, let's fall in love.
The most refined ladybugs do it,
When a gentleman calls.
Moths, in your rugs, do it.
What's the use of moth balls?
Locust, in trees, do it, bees do it,
Even overeducated fleas do it,
Let's do it, let's fall in love.

Refrain 5:
The chimpanzees, in the zoos, do it,
Some courageous kangaroos do it,
Let's do it, let's fall in love.
I'm sure giraffes, on the sly, do it,
Heavy hippopotami do it,
Let's do it, let's fall in love.
Old sloths who hang down from twigs do it,
Though the effort is great.
Sweet guinea pigs do it,
Buy a couple and wait.
The world admits bears, in pits, do it,
Even Pekineses, in the Ritz, do it,
Let's do it, let's fall in love.

* The opening lines of refrain 1 were changed to the familiar "Birds do it, bees do it," etc., when Porter realized that many would find the words "Chinks" and "Japs" offensive.

LET'S MISBEHAVE

(from *Paris*)

Words and Music by
COLE PORTER

In slow fox-trot time

Verse:

You could have___ a great ca - reer,___ and you should.___

On - ly one___ thing stops you, dear,___ you're too good.___

Let's Misbehave - 4 - 1
33309

LONGING FOR DEAR OLD BROADWAY

(from *The Pot of Gold*)

Words and Music by
COLE PORTER

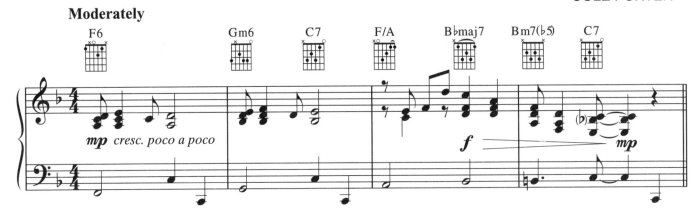

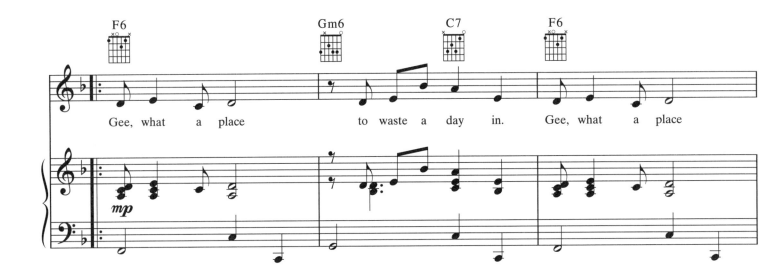

Gee, what a place to waste a day in. Gee, what a place

to fade a-way in. Were I but free, would I could be

Longing for Dear Old Broadway - 3 - 2
33309

LOOKING AT YOU

(from *Wake Up and Dream*)

Words and Music by
COLE PORTER

LOVE FOR SALE

(from *The New Yorkers*)

Words and Music by
COLE PORTER

MISS OTIS REGRETS

(from *Hi Diddle Diddle*)

Words and Music by
COLE PORTER

MISTER AND MISSUS FITCH

(from *Gay Divorce*)

Words and Music by
COLE PORTER

Moderately

Verse:

On a farm far from pleas-ant, no pair was more peas-ant than Mis-ter and Mis-sus Fitch. Their days, each one dull-er, were so lack-ing in col-or, they did-n't know

Mister and Missus Fitch - 4 - 1
33309

Refrain: **Slowly**

NIGHT AND DAY

(from *Gay Divorce*)

Words and Music by
COLE PORTER

Moderately

Like the

mp poco a poco cresc.

Verse:

beat, beat, beat of the tom - tom, when the jun - gle shad - ows fall, like the

tick, tick, tock of the state - ly clock, as it stands a - gainst the wall, like the

184

OLD-FASHIONED GARDEN

(from *Hitchy-Koo of 1919*)

Words and Music by
COLE PORTER

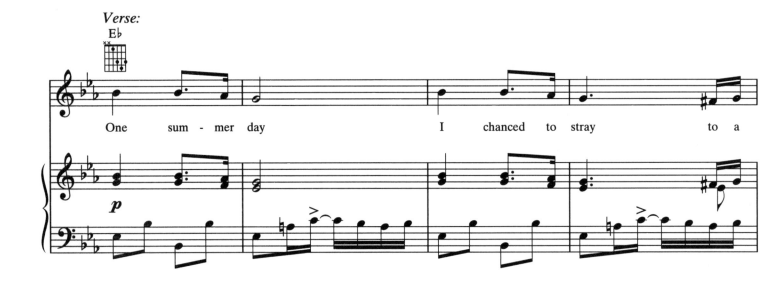

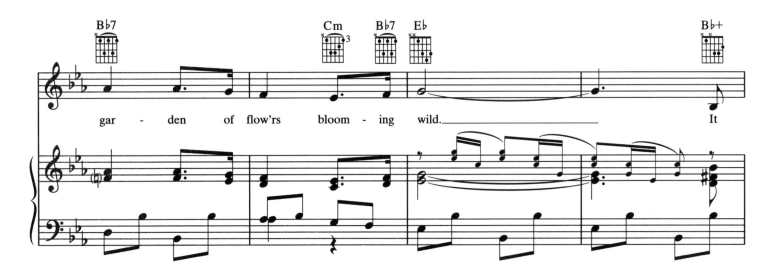

Old-Fashioned Garden - 5 - 1
33309

OURS
(from *Red, Hot and Blue!*)

Words and Music by
COLE PORTER

so man-y bars when we should be un-der the stars, to-geth-er, but a-

lone. Ours is the chance

_ to make ro-mance our own.

With great feeling, but in a steady flowing rhythm

Refrain:

Ours, the white_ Ri-vi-er-a, un-der the moon,

Patter:

She: Don't say "Venice" to me,
Or suggest that old Riviera,
Those faded hot spots fill me with gloom, somehow,
As for a Hindu temple, my pet,
I wouldn't enter one on a bet,
Why I'd be afraid of being chased by a sacred cow.
Don't expect me to dream
Of the silent Sierras, dear,
Or to love that fattening cream
That they give you in Devonshire,
Don't mention the wilds of Paris,
Or, as you call it "gay Paree,"
I may not be right,
But New York is quite
Wild enough for me.

Refrain 2:

She: Ours, the glitter of Broadway, Saturday night,
Ours, a box at the Garden, watching a fight,
Ours, the mad brouhaha of the Plaza's Persian Room,
Or, if this fills you with gloom,
We can go and admire Grant's tomb.
Ours, a home on the river facing the East,
Or on one of Park Avenue's least frightening tow'rs.
All the chat you're chattin'
Sounds to me like Latin,
Why don't we stay in Manhattan
And play, it's all ours.

THE PHYSICIAN
(from *Nymph Errant*)

Words and Music by
COLE PORTER

Once I loved such a shat-ter-ing phy - si - cian, quite the best-look-ing doc-tor in the state. He looked af - ter my phys-i-cal con - di - tion, and his bed - side man-ner was great. When I'd gaze up and see him there a - bove me, look-ing

198

The Physician - 5 - 3
33309

Refrain 2:
He said my cerebellum was brilliant,
And my cerebrum far from N.G.,
I know he thought a lotta
My medulla oblongata,
But he never said he loved me.
He said my maxillaries were marvels,
And found my sternum stunning to see,
He did a double hurdle
When I shook my pelvic girdle,
But he never said he loved me.
He seemed amused
When he first made a test of me
To further his medical art,
Yet he refused,
When he'd fix up the rest of me,
To cure that ache in my heart.
I know he thought my pancreas perfect,
And for my spleen was keen as could be,
He said of all his sweeties,
I'd the sweetest diabetes,
But he never said he loved me.

Refrain 3:
He said my vertebrae were "sehr schöne,"
And called my coccyx "plus que gentil,"
He murmured "molto bella,"
When I sat on his patella,
But he never said he loved me.
He took a fleeting look at my thorax,
And started singing slightly off-key,
He cried, "May Heaven strike us,"
When I played my umbilicus,
But he never said he loved me.
As it was dark,
I suggested we walk about
Before he returned to his post.
Once in the park,
I induced him to talk about
The thing I wanted the most.
He lingered on with me until morning,
Yet when I tried to pay him his fee,
He said, "Why, don't be funny,
It is I who owe you money,"
But he never said he loved me.

RIDIN' HIGH

(from *Red, Hot and Blue!*)

Words and Music by
COLE PORTER

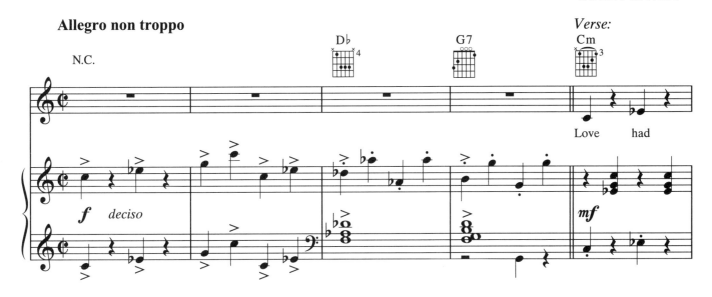

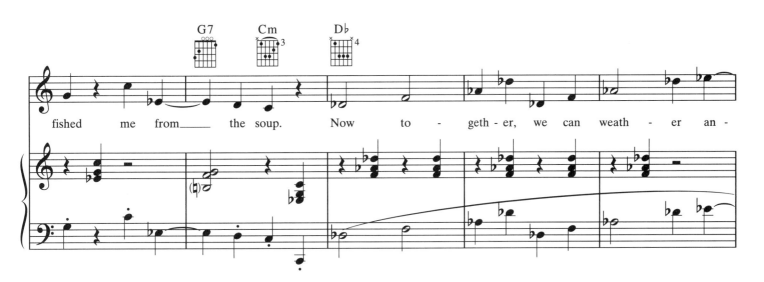

Ridin' High - 5 - 1
33309

TAKE ME BACK TO MANHATTAN

(from *The New Yorkers*)

Words and Music by
COLE PORTER

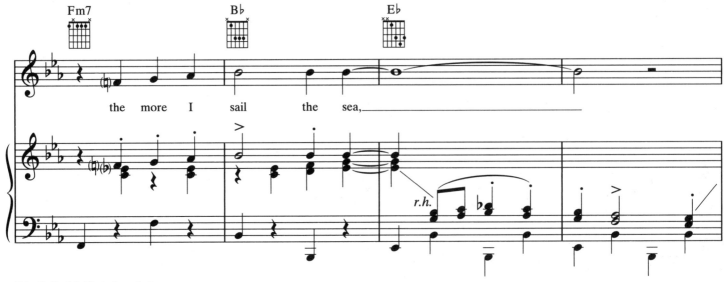

Take Me Back to Manhattan - 5 - 1
33309

WAKE UP AND DREAM

(from *Wake Up and Dream*)

Words and Music by
COLE PORTER

212

A little slower

Refrain:

THEY ALL FALL IN LOVE
(from *The Battle of Paris*)

Words and Music by
COLE PORTER

They All Fall in Love - 5 - 1
33309

THE TALE OF THE OYSTER

(from *Fifty Million Frenchmen*)

Words and Music by
COLE PORTER

YOU DON'T KNOW PAREE

(from *Fifty Million Frenchmen*)

Words and Music by
COLE PORTER

Rubato

Refrain:

Though you've been a - round a lot, and danced a lot, and laughed a lot;

you don't know Pa - ree. You may say you've seen a lot, and

heard a lot, and learned a lot; you don't know Pa - ree.

Pa - ree___ will still be laugh - ing, af - ter ev - 'ry one of us dis - ap -

WEREN'T WE FOOLS?

(written for Fanny Brice)

Words and Music by
COLE PORTER

WHAT IS THIS THING CALLED LOVE?

(from *Wake Up and Dream*)

Words and Music by
COLE PORTER

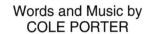

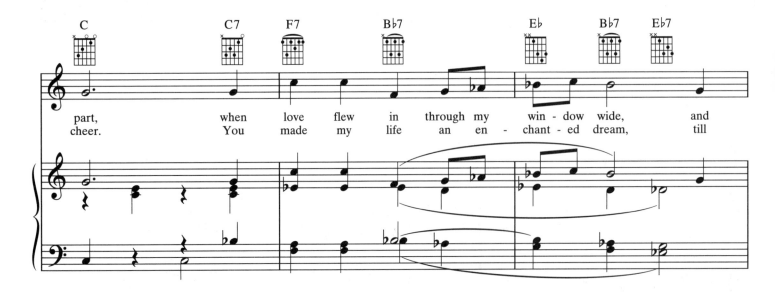

I was a hum-drum per-son, lead-ing a life a-
You gave me days of sun-shine, you gave me nights of

part, when love flew in through my win-dow wide, and
cheer. You made my life an en-chant-ed dream, till

WHERE HAVE YOU BEEN?
(from *The New Yorkers*)

Words and Music by
COLE PORTER

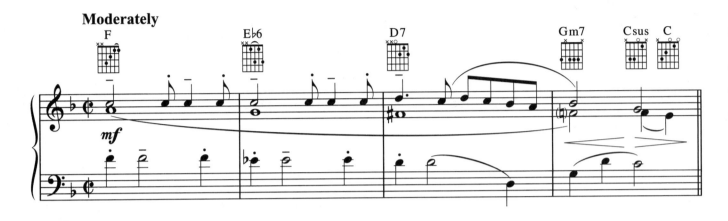

Verse:

If ev-er you love a-gain,___ if such luck could be,

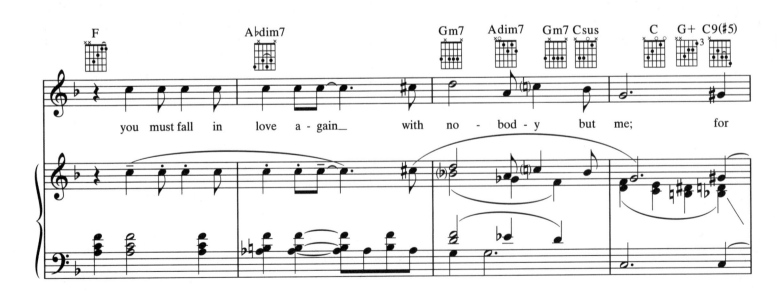

you must fall in love a-gain___ with no-bod-y but me; for

WHICH?

(from *Wake Up and Dream*)

Words and Music by
COLE PORTER

WHY SHOULDN'T I?

(from *Jubilee*)

Words and Music by
COLE PORTER

All my life I've been so se-clud-ed, love has e-lud-ed me. But from

know-ing sec-ond-hand what I do of it, I feel cer-tain I could stand a clos-er

view of it. Till to-day, I stud-ied love dis-creet-ly, but

now that I'm com-plete-ly free, I must find some kind per-so-na

gra-ta to give me da-ta per-son-al-ly.

Slowly, with tender expression

Refrain:

Why should-n't I take a chance when ro-mance pass-es

by? Why should-n't I know of love?

Why Shouldn't I? - 4 - 2
33309

YOU DO SOMETHING TO ME

(from *Fifty Million Frenchmen*)

Words and Music by
COLE PORTER

Verse 2:
If I seem to stray
When you talk this way,
It's because I'm wondering
What I ought to say.
I could cry, please don't,
But I believe I won't,
For when you talk to me
Such a soothing feeling goes through me.

YOU'VE GOT THAT THING

(from *Fifty Million Frenchmen*)

Words and Music by
COLE PORTER

Refrain 2:
You've got that thing, you've got that thing,
That thing that makes vines prefer to cling;
Yes, you've got that thing, that certain thing.
You've got those looks, those fatal looks
That make book censors enjoy their books.
'Cause you've got that thing, that certain thing.
Just what made Samson be, for years,
Delilah's lord and keeper?
She only had a pair of shears,
But you, you've got a reaper.
You've got that pow'r, that pow'r to grip
That makes me map out a wedding trip
For the early spring;
You've got that thing.

Refrain 3:
You've got that thing, you've got that thing,
That thing that makes bees refuse to sting;
Yes, you've got that thing, that certain thing.
You've got that kiss, that kiss that warms,
That makes reformers reform reforms.
'Cause you've got that thing, that certain thing.
They tell us Trojan Helen's lips
Made ev'ry man her slavey.
If her face launched a thousand ships,
Well, yours could launch a navy.
*You've got that love, and such a lot
It makes me think you're prepared for what
Any stork might bring;
You've got that thing.

*Or (last 4 lines): You've ideas inside your head
That make me order an extra bed
With an extra spring;
You've got that thing.

YOU'RE THE TOP

(from *Anything Goes*)

Words and Music by
COLE PORTER

Verse 2:
Your words poetic are not pathetic,
On the other hand, boy, you shine,
And I feel after every line
A thrill divine
Down my spine.
Now gifted humans like Vincent Youmans
Might think that your song is bad,
But for a person who's just rehearsin',
Well, I gotta say this, my lad:

Refrain 3:
You're the top!
You're a Ritz hot toddy.
You're the top!
You're a Brewster body.
You're the boats that glide on the sleepy Zuider Zee,
You're a Nathan panning,
You're Bishop Manning,
You're broccoli.
You're a prize,
You're a night at Coney,
You're the eyes
Of Irene Bordoni.
I'm a broken doll, a fol-de-rol, a blop,
But if, baby, I'm the bottom,
You're the top!

Refrain 4:
You're the top!
You're an Arrow collar.
You're the top!
You're a Coolidge dollar.
You're the nimble tread of the feet of Fred Astaire,
You're an O'Neil drama,
You're Whistler's mama,
You're Camembert.
You're a rose,
You're Inferno's Dante,
You're the nose
Of the great Durante.
I'm just in the way, as the French would say, "De trop,"
But if, baby, I'm the bottom,
You're the top!

Refrain 5:
You're the top!
You're a Waldorf salad.
You're the top!
You're a Berlin ballad.
You're a baby grand of a lady and a gent,
You're an old Dutch master,
You're Mrs. Astor,
You're Pepsodent.
You're romance,
You're the steppes of Russia,
You're the pants on a Roxy usher.
I'm a lazy lout that's just about to stop,
But if, baby, I'm the bottom,
You're the top!

Refrain 6:
You're the top!
You're a dance in Bali.
You're the top!
You're a hot tamale.
You're an angel, you, simply too, too, too diveen,
You're a Boticcelli,
You're Keats,
You're Shelly,
You're Ovaltine.
You're a boom,
You're the dam at Boulder,
You're the moon over Mae West's shoulder.
I'm the nominee of the G.O.P., or GOP,
But if, baby, I'm the bottom,
You're the top!

Refrain 7:
You're the top!
You're the Tower of Babel.
You're the top!
You're the Whitney Stable.
By the River Rhine, you're a sturdy stein of beer,
You're a dress from Saks's,
You're next year's taxes,
You're stratosphere.
You're my thoist,
You're a Drumstick Lipstick,
You're da foist
In da Irish Svipstick,
I'm a frightened frog that can find no log to hop,
But if, baby, I'm the bottom,
You're the top!